# Rabbits, Poets & Puppets

The Thoughts & Observations of a Few

horrific truths & beautiful lies

**collected poems by**
**Vincent Convertito**
**&**
**Thomas Koch**

*AuthorHouse™ LLC*
*1663 Liberty Drive*
*Bloomington, IN 47403*
*www.authorhouse.com*
*Phone: 1-800-839-8640*



*Published by AuthorHouse 04/22/2014*

*ISBN: 978-1-4969-0328-0 (sc)*
*ISBN: 978-1-4969-0327-3 (e)*

*This book is printed on acid-free paper.*

The first installment in a series of previously unpublished and new poetry collected from the thoughts and observations of Vincent Convertito and Thomas Koch.

## acknowledgments

*(to undergo revision)*

*for Christy who introduced me to all of her friends at the party as a writer*

*feel free to visit us at*

rabbitspoetsandpuppets.com

*& write to us at*

rabbitspoetsandpuppets@gmail.com

cut the strings of a puppet me

let me fall

will learn to walk

what will I say?

**RPP**

## Contents

### ONE

## TWO

## THREE

## FOUR

# PART ONE

## islands of thought

## the cabinet

the cabinet
above my sitting room fireplace
is the smallest space
in the house
yet I check it
nearly every day.

Sometimes a smell
foreign or foul
begins in that room
and I'll immediately check
the cabinet
anticipating a mouse, a rat,
or maybe a dead bat-
something that made its way
through the center stack chimney.
It could even be
a wet spot

from rain drops
that eventually
let gravity
lead them to the first floor.

Sometimes it's only habit.
I'll open it
and forget the reason
for bothering the
antique hinge.

But I'm never sorry
regardless of the discovery
simply because
it's the least complicated part of my home.
A crooked square
full of fascinating detail
and more mystery
than a book

**welcome**

like us,

letters & words

lay out

arrange themselves

wish understanding

& welcome

like us, letters & words

paint pictures

worth more

than a thousand

worlds;

alphabet characters,

people- possibilities

seemingly endless--

a fullmoon

on a fine nite, beautiful

strangers everywhere,

infinite imagination, manifesting

itself, round & sharp!

ink conglomerates, bodies

born, rest

scattered seeds upon earthly pages

precise, measured

people, ink

obeying gravity, making a home

5 x 8 worlds

vast white oceans surrounding islands of thought

fish & meaning swim, live deep

below surface

people, poems; words on paper
inked out, truthing their way
across pages of life. people, poems
metaphors knock on doors, open hearts

reach for more... hidden between letters
of words, meaning lay naked-
a beautiful stranger
never alone; trees,
flowers life somewhere &
everywhere in the middle of all this,

## I want to ride a motorcycle

but I'm afraid of the bees.

I'm afraid of the one

bee, buzzing across the stretch

of highway

at the exact moment

when I will cross

his b-line path

at eighty miles an hour.

And my sunglasses

will offer no protection

from the terrible impact;

an explosion of yellow and black

and blood

across the entire section

of my right cheek bone

and at the last moment

the stinger will

inject

deeply

into the tender skin

and only seconds

remain

before the constricting swell

takes over my whole face

as if

someone tied flesh pillows

around my head

**it's going to be**

It's going to be
a four cylinder
anyway.

And you'll have to read
my other poem
about gas prices
and the cost of
burning
for a further explanation.
Anyway,
this four cylinder
will tow
a pick-up truck, a dog, and me
across the country
before my fortieth birthday.
I'm going to visit
people I've never met.

**what will you accomplish within one year from this date?**

“things to do tomorrow,” he thought.
“things to do tomorrow and the day
after that. things to do forever.

which is fine,” he thought,
“so long as I want to do these things
as badly as they need to be done.”

a smile accompanied the thought
and eyes lit up. overhead loomed
thin crooked branches weighed
down by apples. one apple

in particular stood out, it was not
the worst looking apple
nor was it close to perfect

but this apple seemed closer

or more real next to the other

still delicious apples

each hanging ecstatically, bouncing

as he tugged softly on just one.

## cotton candy

the smell of cotton candy-
blue & sticky- sweet like the suckers
who will pay a few extra dollars
for the ring toss

a beyond-oversized turquoise teddy bear
that the wrong-for-each-other
teenage crushes will win

the trampled green grass and garbage cans
overflowing, spilling well over everywhere
thousands of sodas sold & pizzas sliced

fried dough & a carnival
will attract all walks of life-
the elderly couple holding hands,
a panicking mother

momentarily separated

from her six year old

the hobos looming

like the Ferris wheel

scratching the night sky

scraping the walls

of ten o clock in july

## coffee and a barn

I've come

to the conclusion

that aspirin, wine and golf

don't help.

As a matter

of fact

I've carefully

narrowed down

the remedy

for being an overworked

and under-appreciated

father.

It is a coffee

and a barn.

In there

among

the lawn mowing machine
and weed whacker with a tin foil throttle
sits the stack of wood.
A great big pile of fresh fuel,
a pile of something
our wives know little about.

The heavy scent of gasoline, oil,
and bags of fertilizer
rest impatiently
inside the chambers
of my “to do” list
and suddenly
the tag sale radio
begins to flow
an old Guns N’ Roses tune.

It’s times like these
that men become
one with

the single speaker

and get goose bumps

of nostalgia.

These aren't the kind of goose bumps

which signal an oncoming bowel movement.

These are the goose bumps

of how we used

to play

in the neighborhood

on bikes

in old tennis shoes, wet from the day before

and a bag of Twizzlers

barely clinging to our back pocket.

These are the goose bumps

which remind us

of just how far

we've come.

A coffee, a barn

and few moments

to accept reality.

**ten things I never wanted but somehow, like a shit magnet, managed to inherit at one point or another:**

cancer

poison ivy

allergic bee stings

blood poisoning

an asshole for an aunt

debt

allergies

stress

a commute

commitments

## someone tell me

who whispered what

to Michelangelo

so long ago

that let him chip

away ever so

diligently silent,

arduously soft

throughout the

cool, cool nights

& into sun drenched

mornings, blonde

beams of light

warming wooden

planks blanketed in

flakes snow white

## consider the wrinkles

consider the wrinkles
forming in weathered
hands of an aging man
stuck always outside

study the un-manicured
nails- permanently dirty-
fingers slightly curled,
his palm facing up,
waiting for some change

watch as a silver coin
drops, as sunlight reflects
off of Washington's face

observe a crooked yellow
grin that forms a "thank you"

concentrate on the white

stubble that grows on his chin-

notice the nicotine stained mustache

that covers a thin cracked lip...

know that the stranger who is hungry

was a child, still a man

**If he only knew**

I googled you, Grandpa

and saw

the State Street Hardware store

from satellite

in a blurry blip

lust like

my memories

of our times together

in your apartment

**fish bowl**

these 3 golden girls

walk to & fro- the same worn

99 tiles beneath their feet

the idle shuffle of their swim

as food is lowered into their tank

old gills take another languid breath

a large, leafy green plant

decorates the corner-

red tape at eye level

reminds us all

of the glass

**feng shui**

The master
says an octagon
for your space
like an office or bedroom or kitchen
is key
but
who's got time
to turn
a crooked room
in a crooked house
with a crooked back
into a cure?
I certainly do not
even have the time to think
about the proper place
for a plant
with broad green leaves.

"It's a simple life fix"

the masters

tell you

in books

and television shows.

But I always wonder.

If it's so easy

why doesn't everybody

cure

their space?

And for those who do,

I honestly haven't noticed

their natural octagon energy

flowing from anything

other than

the typical

bullshit

streaming

in high definition

from the flat screen

or more commonly

their mouths.

## The biggest mistake

The biggest mistake
was leaving my wife in charge
of the fire.
And now
I've got
something we like to call character
permanently burnt
into the hardwood floor.
It isn't something
I can easily hide
or repair
or buff out with some wax.
Instead
it's become our own
natural piece of art
that takes on a new meaning
depending on how much wine I've drunk.
Oh, it still gets me

every time I open the door

like a cow left one of his spots

in the open space of my kitchen

except it's fucking ugly

and dark

and depressing when I'm sober.

But as the evening progresses

and I loosen up

I see an elephant trunk

or a cornucopia

or even the shape of my penis

right there

in front of the stove

in front of the hearth

in front of my face

each time I reload.

**crazy how midnight**

crazy how midnight
squeezes the truth
from lips, how stars
whisper secrets
into the ears of anyone
who will listen

chilling is the wisdom
carried on autumn breezes,
wondrous are thoughts
freely falling from trees

not just any fool believes
a moonlit patio remembers
stories told by two tall
glasses of red, red wine

**I go late to bed**

Just the Cicadas
are making noise
at this horrible hour
when everything is out
including my dogs.

# PART TWO

## amidst the smell of gasoline

## Thanks, Allie

Thanks, Allie,

for the Cheerio bomb

you left between

my sheets.

I discovered it

near three a.m.

thinking it was

a terrible spider

crawling up my

hamstring

near the lower part of my ass cheek.

Just so you know,

I jumped

like a little bitch

taking all the covers with me

to the floor.

Mommy was pissed
and moaning
and asking what the hell was up.

"There's a fuckin' spider in the bed." I said.

And proceeded to shake
everything violently
until I was sure it was gone.

Trying to repair
what was left of the night
I sprawled naked
once again
below the newly organized
covers
only to discover
this time it was making its way up my back.

In one fluid motion

like a highly trained ninja

I rolled and slapped

the mattress

with an open palm thud

fatally wounding a single Cheerio.

## perhaps it was the moon

Perhaps it was the moon-
rusted orange and round-
that made him do it.
That made him drive
so fast to her house.

A perfect autumn moon
hanging low in the sky,
just beginning its rise
into the evening, could easily
have been the culprit.

Hell, it could've been
anybody but himself,
he thought through
a quick right turn
that led straight
into acceleration.

Leaves scattered

and were strewn about

as the car hurried past them,

blowing both gold and red

leaves far from the ones

they had slowly fallen

next to all throughout

the long cold day.

He was jealous of the leaves.

They simply wait, he thought,

until something other than themselves

changes their situation.

A cool breeze will always invite leaves

to dance when the wind decides to blow.

What choice does a leaf have

but to enjoy the song played?

The red and gold leaves had rested
silently until he roared past them.

Their sleep interrupted means nothing
or everything as his thoughts
blow around, swirl about the mind.

The leaves, he feels, are much like him.

Not sad to fall from their tree,
rather anxious.

## theme of red

Billy blushed; red cheeks

had no idea that show

& tell would go so well

as all the kids grew

wide-eyed in awe;

the shiny metal sat so

heavy in his tiny hands;

a small thumb slid back a lock

thrilled was he who then

showed the class just how

fast the bullets could fly

## Excuse me, Mr. President

Excuse me, Mr. President,

while I take a break

from the debt crisis

and ask a more

critical question:

Who the fuck

hack-saws

his own kid's head off

for

Mom to see?

Are you kidding me?

Like saving a small portion

of the 15 trillion

is going to make me feel

any better
about anything.

Listen,
the better plan
is to allow me
to raise my family
and you could help dearly
by shutting your arrogant pie hole.

Let the good people live.

And fuck you, Jeremiah White.

**Shoes**

Rumored protection

Fashionable cages
In which we
Unnecessarily
Cram our feet

As to separate us
From the animals

The way a classroom
Is strapped like a helmet
Onto the mind of the child

Who would otherwise roam free

**I tell my students there is much to write about. "Stare at the bark of a tree, kids. Eventually it will become a poem."**

I'm a rotten man.

There is no poem

in the bark

or

in the sun

or

in the scratch

on your mom's dining room table.

I just don't have

the guts

to tell them

the poem is inside

the tangled grief of our lives.

I just don't have the heart

to tell them

the poem will never come

to most of them

because only the poets

are brave enough

to untangle

everything.

Only the poets

are brave enough

to spill their guts.

I don't have the heart

to tell them

that most

will continue

with life

until that knotted mass

reaches a point

where it can never become undone.

I don't have the guts

to tell them

that my poem

will eventually be

like their

heart attack.

**bowties**

I wore a tie to the job I wore
for more years than I like to admit
like a professional should

but I do admit that every now
& then I had the urge
to take scissors to the tie;
to cut it off mid-chest, in mid conversation
or mid lecture & by every now
& then I mean a lot of the time

if not all of the time. & there were
days that my students watched in awe
as the scissors did all of the talking

& a helpless bulk of a trendy plaid
or paisley tie would fall to the floor-

there were many paisley messes
to clean- silk blood and silk funerals

funny how the tie was still around
my neck but it didn't bother me
as much anymore knowing that I had
slain the dragon half of that mess

makes me wonder why I didn't
do it more often
or at least
wear the custom-tailored ties regularly

who knows- maybe a bow tie was the way
to go from the start for a guy like me

nah-
then I'd just be confirming our suspicions
that I was a graduate from clown college

## In Response to a NY Times Article on Naming the Runaway Cobra at the Bronx Zoo

It's a stupid idea

to run a contest

about naming

a baby cobra

who escaped

from the zoo.

It's true,

snakes hide all the time

and you know the rules-

if we name one

we'll have to name them all.

Could you imagine

how many cobras

will be lined up

at town halls

across the world

demanding their individual recognition?
what will you do to stop
the massive protest?
That's right,
nothing,
because these things
are poisonous
and pissed off most of the time
and looking
for a reason
to fight,
let me guess,
you'd get a bunch of those dudes
to play the little flute thing
and make all of these cobras
go home?
Not a chance in hell
besides
Indiana Jones
is a fictional movie

and a fictional character

and when push comes to shove

the truth is

cobras are bad ass.

So bad ass

a Sylvester Stallone

movie was named

after the title character

and he was a rogue cop.

You think you're ready to start

a mess

like this?

## guys shouldn't wear ankle bracelets

If you've got a cock

that hangs

or looks like a wad

between your legs

Speedos are ok.

But an ankle bracelet is gay.

Even a homo shouldn't sport

something that jingles

every time you take a step;

it just accentuates

the limp nature of your ways.

Can you imagine

chilling with the boys

on a winter's eve

a few pops of wine and beer

maybe even a whiskey

and your best friend decides

he's going to light a fire

to take the snap outta the air.
And the lot of you
like a pack of sled dogs
race towards the barn
where the cord of firewood is kept
and the walk-behind power mower
and weed whacker
and chainsaw hibernate
amidst the smell of
gasoline, turpentine, and testosterone.
Each one of you wants to swing the axe
like Paul Bunyon

as if you're Mr. Backwoodsman in the flesh
but you'll never get a turn
because the whole thing sours
in a flash
when Paul picks up the axe
seemingly affected by its weight
his wrist barely able to hold the handle

and his grip not even causing veins

to pop from the backside of his hand

almost like it's a lollipop

he's about to suck instead of chop.

The rest of you

stare, deciding whether you know him or not

and he kneels, careful to sweep nearby debris

saving his khakis

and during the whole process

his pants

edge up from the tight, squat position

only to reveal a low cut pair of

argyle socks

and his ankle bone sticks out like a rock.

That's when you notice the shiny,

interlaced twine of bracelet

dangling just above his slip-on shoes.

You won't stay

to witness the rubbery arm swing,

the kind where the axe bounces off the top

of a thoroughly dried piece of ash

because you're not ready

to admit

your best friend wears an ankle bracelet.

Somehow you know you'll always be

associated with it, too.

## Thirty-Three

Tonight

I was set to write

a poem

yet

found myself

erasing

line

after line

after line

until it occurred

to me

that I

was the one

with the bigger problem.

**of**

return the moon to its corner

save a sliver of exactness of

fullness of yesternight

pour out the stars- scattered

exactly, they fall into their place-

the clockwork of the universe

# PART THREE

## this morning
## is a vast blue ocean

**windows, bridges and doors:**

not enough bridges being built
with stones these days-
stones dragged for miles
to create a safer passage...

stones would certainly
make it much harder for
the fool to burn bridges...

doors are good for secrets
and such- keep skeletons
inside of their closets,
keep locksmiths in business

doors certainly provide
us with more room to hide
ourselves in than the
treasure chest ever did

windows- so easy to look

out and see in to...

the eyes of the home

the bridge to the outside

the door I never with curtains

close when it snows

**woodstove, wine and snow**

As far as I'm concerned

three things make a man.

There isn't much else to argue about that.

Define a man

however you wish,

but I challenge you

to find

a more content

son of a bitch

than the peaceful drunk

sitting at his kitchen table,

full magnum,

flames rising,

and a mountain of white

just outside his window.

Nowhere to go

except in his mind.

From there,

well,

he can go anywhere

and that's more than I can say for most.

## see the poem

snow falls from a Boston sky-
flakes work their way down on the busy city,
a half moon tries to outshine
changing lights and whizzing cars.

but the poems are everywhere.

the bicycles chained to posts, slowly cloaked
in this evening's magic; misadventure waiting
to happen as a scarf wrapped lover unlocks
his best means of reaching his better half

the footsteps that tell stories-
their sizes and stride distinct, their direction
known and lost, trampled over,
covered quietly
the cars never stop, quickly shaking
the slush on the black path home.

aged stonework has never been colder.
resilient in the night,
the steeple is taller than usual.
the weathervane resists accumulation
and the iron handles of the clock
keep tick ticking.

the bicycles surrender,
give in to soft white mystery.

the tracks get deeper.
and some things never change.

the cars keep their pace
and the high heeled women
complain of New England weather

the lights keep changing
and everything else is the same…
the snow falls and the footsteps are buried.

new ones take their place;

their destination undecided.

a weathervane laughs

and the clock keeps time.

cars keep their pace on the black path home.

**lawn chairs in winter**

Oil prices
have gone through
the roof
and so does the heat
with temperatures down
and thermostats up.

What the fuck?
I've had to keep
that little round
dial
set at sixty
with a freezing child
and a freezing wife
a freezing pantry and
freezing pipes.

I'm feeding my stove
log after log, after log, after log
and waking
at heinous hours
in the morning
to keep her going
because the goddamn kitchen
has no reliable
source of heat.

And to top it all off
the shit hit the fan on the eighteenth of
January,
after a long day of work,
I can home to find
the bottled up dogs
had bottled up bladders
and all of their shivering
must have caused them
to explode

and the piss

traveled with gravity

across the crooked floors

and found its way

underneath chair legs,

underneath the base of the cabinets,

underneath my daughter's plastic kitchenette.

I stepped in it.

I swear

the terrible mess

was

on the verge

of congealing.

I think I saw

crystallization.

The floor was an ice cube.

The fire was out.

And the groceries I lugged in

were carefully placed
on top of it all.

I did the next best thing.
I threw out the groceries
in a heated rage
wasted an entire roll of paper towel
sprayed a gallon of Windex
and ordered a large bacon and olive pie.

The familiar beep
of the kitchen door alarm
went off
and so did my wife's mouth
and so did my daughter's leg
and in a flurry
of activity
one of them said,
"What's wrong, Daddy?"

After three fast glasses

of red wine, a near record spike

in my blood pressure, possible frostbite

and palms covered in dog piss

I cordially responded

with a believable,

"Nothing."

**the mind is a puddle**

the mind

is a puddle

or a million drops of thought collected

the mind

is a think tank; brimful always

the mind

is a many channeled television

full of images, contrived and real;

horrific truths and beautiful lies

the mind

is a deck of cards always in need

of the occasional reshuffling

the mind

is a sophisticated watch

composed of many small parts,

tiny metal gears that can't help

but to tell time

the mind

is a flower

whose petals will fall

## Play a Song Without the Music and it Sucks

Coffee is the morning music

and laughter

is the chorus

throughout

the working day.

Wine

is the guitar solo

of my evening

which carries me

to the poem,

to the bed.

Life sucks

without

the music.

**spiral staircase**
**(i want our brains to touch)**

strike a match and light a candle
take a midnight stroll across
the gardens of my mind

walk slowly
down the stone corridors
of my brain-
look at all the paintings
i've hung on the castle walls

keep the candle lit

follow any well worn rug
along the hallways of memory-
visit them again and again

come stand where i've always stood-

see the world from the balcony

of my eyes

poke around and open doors

uncover sleeping secrets

and ignore the dragon-

he guards nothing anymore

take the spiral stair case

down to my heart

and blow out the candle

**this morning is a vast blue ocean**

a teddy bear I've become
trapped happily under the feathery

weight of your dreaming arm;
the softest anchor, slowly rising and

falling with the rolling waves of my heartbeat.
this morning is a vast blue ocean

and your body a most thoughtfully designed
vessel docking safely in my harbor where

I am teddy bear with brilliant vision,
microscopic eyes and under lens are

eyelashes, each and every one, I could
count them like reasons, so many

lashes, each distinct and to think
I never saw them like this- 1000x

more real, but a teddy bear is me
peering out from the observatory

of my heart where millimeters may be
light years and each freckle pronounced,

seen clearly worlds away; freckles arranged
like constellations in the heavens resting softly

on your cheek- stars aligned just right-
pointing the way as I'd fly forever to be home,

tucked comfortably like sheets of answers
beneath the paperweight of your embrace-

a philosophical teddy bear with adoring
eyes wonderfully wondering how it is so

that each hair falling across your face

creates a somehow sunset on this

vast ocean and what it must mean

that you smile while you sleep

**love poem number eighty three**

I *can*

count the ways

I love you.

It's

eighty two

to be exact.

In fact

every time I tried to write

about you

I thought of something new

and better

to say

like the way

you feel

when you're asleep

and I press myself

warmly up

against the half-moon curve of your back

and my heart
stretches
beyond its limits
and kisses
every rhythmic beat
of yours.

I can
count the ways
I love you
and would have
written more
but decided to stop.
Counting.
Not because
I ran out of reasons!
Instead,
I wanted to spend more minutes with you
and besides
if all of the reasons
ever had to be printed

I'd be responsible
for killing the trees
and destroying our planet
which would mean
no place
for our hearts
to mess around
at night
after we fall
asleep.

And for the record
number 17
is just three words
long.

So
damn
beautiful

## a mediocre poem for the generic love interest in your life when you have to play it cool

your eyes are like most eyes;

almond shaped with a familiar

medium brown color.

your eyelashes

are about an inch long

& that does not upset me

## sell fish

only sometimes do I know how badly

you so selfishly hurt me & it happens

when I sometimes wistfully wish

you an awkward life selling fish;

rotten, fishy fish on a slippery pier

## ape shit

I'd go bananas

if you

nonchalantly

came home

and sucked

my cock.

## the red wheel barrel of my mind

sorry I had

to close the doors.

but don't worry;

you'll never see

what you've missed.

only a smile...

the same one

everyone receives;

the cover to a book

I'll never let you

read

# PART FOUR

## igniting the grand finale

## I saw a lion

I saw a lion in a cat
that sat on a windowsill
trapped behind
glass

I watched
until she watched me
a pensive gaze indeed

I sat parked
stuck in a truck
in line at a stop sign

what did the lion
see in me?

**just a ball of wax**

If I ever contracted rabies
my friends would be rich
because I'd auction off the footage
on ebay to the highest bidder.
It would start with the paralysis,
then to the twitching and foam
ultimately
to me
naked
propped in one of those cool
aluminum lawn chairs
right in the center of my own backyard
and I'm not sure who it would be
but one of my friends
would have the honors of
igniting the grand finale;
a few sparklers in my ass
the garden hose full blast

spurting from between my legs like

a powerful piss

and a stuffed animal dressed like a raccoon

biting my ankle.

The film would continue like this

with Frank Sinatra's *"My Way"*

blaring from the outdoor speakers.

It would end with a terrible pistol shot

and my forehead would explode into

a million pieces.

It would have to stay that way, too.

For at least a few hours anyway

**what if**

storm after violent storm,
unpredictable weather patterns;
forecasters forced to retire early.
all we know is what not to expect.

kids making money by being brave-
running the last few feasible errands.
no one wants to leave home.

windows are shattered or boarded up.
trees uprooted or fallen, roads flooded.
hail balls rule the day
uncertainty reigns at night...

rescue teams can't dispatch
radios down, communication limited
to messengers in makeshift armor who dare
travel about a land under weather attack.

umbrellas are a joke.

raincoats are barely maybe adequate

for an hour or two, no more.

businesses closed. school cancelled.

hope you like where you live.

families finally get to know one another...

*stock in wax would skyrocket*

*if there were still a market.*

candles light another corner of a room

where meetings are held...

*what to do, can anyone*

*manufacture more candles?*

make a wish...

but don't tell anyone

**apple sauce**

even apples come with stickers
and such to prove its newness
and perhaps need to be returned...

I eat my apple with its sticker on
the way a kid keeps the tag on his lid
because I'm fresh like that...

I eat an apple like a steak.
I make a meal out it; a silver fork,
a sharp knife- takes me half an hour...

sometimes I leave my apple out
on the counter after having slowly,
carefully bitten off all the skin
so that it browns up over night

then in the morning I have a nice

new apple with its own weird

new skin wrapped around it…

under that skin is a perfectly good,

hardly used apple.

*Low miles*, I like to say.

## point of procrastination

perhaps

procrastination has a point

to all of its waiting

like the perfect line

in a perfect poem

or a perfect rhyme

between two strangers

who discover

each other.

besides

who wants to mow the lawn

anyway?

## golfing

I tried it.

I sucked.

I quit.

## expiration dates:
## twenty-one words or less

### 1

we have been shelved-

our stories embedded in the barcode

you star as the main ingredient

somewhere is an expiration date

### 2

as a gambler I take great pride

in eating food after their expiration dates;

the porcelain throne

my craps table

### 3

good, bad, ugly, rich;

we all eventually expire...

candles return (us) to dark

footprints in the sand

are born to disappear

## death must feel

death must feel

somehow

like déjà vu

eerily familiar

strangely horrifically

perfectly brilliant

how familiar the white lights

of death

must feel

**last will and testicle**

Please arrange

for a party

of envelope lickers

on the day of my burial

so that they may

see to my final request.

Make sure they are

seated,

around a portable poker table covered in vinyl,

outside

in foldable chairs

sealing letters

to random addresses

and Kool and The Gang

must play

from a boom box-

cassette tape only-

weather not permitting.

Xerox

at least one hundred copies

of the following note

with a dollar bill

stapled to the corner:

"I would have sent four quarters, but I'm afraid of the weight. Use this dollar the next time you encounter one of those machines with a gripping claw and try to win a prize."

Let them all know

I was

always so close

to holding everything

I ever wanted

but somehow

I feel

that life is rigged

to the point

that no matter

how much luck is on your side

even the most meaningless treasure

seems to slip away

just before

## holiday

I'll have a party

to celebrate all of my friends

and it won't cost more than

two bottles of wine

for myself

and a couple of dog biscuits

for the best damn black mutt

sixty bucks

could ever buy.

**my life is a poem**

with a black lab sprawled

& sleeping by the back door

a fire still lit

two empty bottles of wine

on the table

my life is a poem

one long poem

that'll ramble on

well after

a post-midnight

bedtime

## just so you know

just so you know

this poem was written

after I already wrote two

and that is a lot of poems for one night.

But as you may already know

the poems will continue

to get less important

as the heavy night

begins to wear

the passion

down to

size.

**the song of myself**

Thank you, Mr. Whitman

For providing me

An opportunity to

Yawp.

And now, I humbly wish

To tell

My song

With your permission.

( silence)

(waiting)

(a sound, a form of communicative reply from

the deceased Whitman granting my request)

My song

is

sometimes invisible to your ears

because you're listening with your eyes

and it hurts

but I cannot

force any of you to understand

my song.

My song

often misses a beat

when my heart skips

and the rifts

between us grow

to the point

my song is an echo.

To be cliché,

my song is

an unfinished symphony

of words and rhythms

a prism of everything noisy

yet to be organized

always growing longer

and sometimes stronger

nevertheless

playing

as the great equalizer

ultimately will mix

it

and my song will end.

Till then,

my song remains.

## About the Authors

Thomas Koch is a poetry enthusiast, published poet and poetry teacher. Those closest to him, however, know that Thomas' culinary skills rival his prose; in particular is his well sought after recipe for chicken paprikash. A veteran English teacher at a public school in Fairfield County, Thomas has converted his red barn into a studio for both writing and wood working projects. Many writing sessions for *Rabbits, Poets & Puppets* took place in the barn as well as in his wood burning stove-warmed kitchen. Thomas lives in Trumbull, CT in a haunted colonial that dates back to the 1790's. He lives with his females and wood piles.

Vincent Convertito is a published poet, a recipient of the Leo Connellan Prize for poetry and pursuing a MFA in creative writing. When he's not visiting his friends and family in Connecticut, he's looking ahead to his next travel adventure—ideally involving a passport. As a former English teacher, Vincent especially misses working on creative writing and poetry with young writers and he welcomes the chance to work with such groups again. For money, he auctions himself out to the highest bidder, generously accepting more opportunities to remind himself that he doesn't wish to do tile and stone work any longer unless explicitly for the thrill of it. Vincent currently resides in Shelton, CT where he's encouraged to follow his dreams of writing and travel thanks to well placed post-it notes about his charmingly small cape.

Convertito and Koch grew up just a few miles from one another and ran in similar circles but the two did not cross paths until, in the grand scheme of things, just recently. Their eventual collaboration can be credited to several memorable encounters where it became known that the two shared a desire to write but it would still be many months before the two actually sat down at Koch's kitchen table to discuss their works—over a bottle or two of the house wine—with one another. Working exclusively on *Rabbits, Poets & Puppets* (RPP) was the result of many work shop sessions where the two wanted to create new works but found themselves discussing older, previously unpublished works that begged their attention. In 2012, Convertito had selected from and arranged the dozens of poems they had each submitted and presented it to Koch as a 4 part book with 52 poems in total. From there, the two have realized only time and money can slow them down . . .

Look for more books coming soon, soon, soon from RPP.